The Gray Ghost of the Confederacy: The Life and Legacy of John Mosby

By Jeffery Mitchell and Charles River Editors

Mosby during the Civil War

About Charles River Editors

Charles River Editors provides superior editing and original writing services across the digital publishing industry, with the expertise to create digital content for publishers across a vast range of subject matter. In addition to providing original digital content for third party publishers, we also republish civilization's greatest literary works, bringing them to new generations of readers via ebooks.

Sign up here to receive updates about free books as we publish them, and visit Our Kindle Author Page to browse today's free promotions and our most recently published Kindle titles.

Introduction

John Singleton Mosby (1833-1916)

"Our poor country has fallen a prey to the conqueror. The noblest cause ever defended by the sword is lost. The noble dead that sleep in their shallow though honored graves are far more fortunate than their survivors. I thought I had sounded the profoundest depth of human feeling, but this is the bitterest hour of my life." – John Mosby

The Civil War is best remembered for the big battles and the legendary generals who fought on both sides, like Robert E. Lee facing off against Ulysses S. Grant in 1864. In kind, the Eastern theater has always drawn more interest and attention than the West. However, while massive armies marched around the country fighting each other, there were other small guerrilla groups that engaged in irregular warfare on the margins, and perhaps the most famous of them was Colonel John Mosby.

Mosby, the "Gray Ghost" of the Confederate lore that celebrates the Lost Cause, has an image that has proven nearly impossible to corrupt or change, and time has done little good against it. Unlike the vanished 19th century code of honor that he represented, Mosby has retained the image and all its connotations; evident in the pictures taken of him in his Confederate uniform and historical portrayals of him, whether they were written just after the Civil War or much later. But that image, which he helped fashioned, was mostly an invention. Mosby styled himself a "Knight of the South", as other Virginians would do during the war, branding himself as a warrior of a culture who obeyed an unspoken code of honor. He defended women and lived by his word. Even the style of combat he chose conformed to the definition of honor that Southerners held. With repeated charges into the ranks of federal cavalry, Mosby was lionized by a culture that gloried in the acts of heroic violence. As the war dragged on, Mosby claimed to fight a style of war that was honorable, but if the Union ever entered into acts he considered uncivilized, he was never beyond revenge, including notorious summary executions of prisoners of war. He was so reviled in the North that rumors quickly spread that Mosby knew of John Wilkes Booth's conspiracy to assassinate Lincoln, and that he may have even assisted in it.

While the South would come to idolize "Southern gentlemen" as epitomized by Robert E. Lee, Mosby operated under a far different nature. Though he enlisted with the Confederate army in Virginia after Fort Sumter, he ultimately left the infantry to join J.E.B. Stuart's cavalry, and he later became infamous as an irregular scout leading a group of rangers around Virginia. Of course, the successful feats of daring that Mosby would accomplish during the war, which included capturing a Union general and riding around behind enemy lines to raid and destroy supplies, were supported by the people of Virginia, thus legitimizing his unconventional move to leave army life. Mosby not only earned the nickname "Gray Ghost" by being elusive, he was so successful that part of Virginia was known as "Mosby's Confederacy" during the war, despite the presence of massive Union armies nearby.

Mosby did all this while looking the part of a diminutive man, a physical appearance that Southern culture did not generally view as masculine. In fact, his small size, just 5'8 and 125 pounds, might actually have provoked his aggression. Either way, Mosby overcame and looked the part as a cavalier on a horse, weathered by the elements and war but never beaten down by the enemy he looked down upon from his mount. *The Gray Ghost of the Confederacy* chronicles the life of Mosby, as well as his Civil War record and legacy. Along with pictures of important people, places, and events, you will learn about the Gray Ghost like never before, in no time at all.

The Gray Ghost of the Confederacy: The Life and Legacy of John Mosby

About Charles River Editors

Introduction

Chapter 1: Mosby's Virginia

Young Mosby

"She is out of the Union now. Virginia is my mother, God bless her! I can't fight against my mother, can I?"[1] - John S. Mosby upon learning of Virginia's secession.

John Singleton Mosby belonged to the ancestral soil of Virginia, both his parents having come from long farming generations in the state who helped found the Old Dominion as a colony and participated in its growth as the dominant state of the slaveholding South. However, Mosby's father never had more than three slaves, and his family belonged to the middling classes of the yeomen farmers that worked the lands between hills and streams, where the mostly loose soils of limestone and eroded granites supported the crops of wheat, hemp, and tobacco. He later recalled in his memoirs, "I recollect that one day I went with my father to our peach orchard on a high ridge, and he pointed out Monticello, the home of Thomas Jefferson, on a mountain a few miles away, and told me some of the history of the great man who wrote the Declaration of

---

[1] Ramage, *Gray Ghost*, 32.

Independence."

The younger Mosby's contact with farm work might have been much more intimate and physical if not for his frail condition at birth and his physical weakness during his youth. At an early age, the physical appearance that most people considered frail and small proved to be a challenge in life, and when he was elderly, Mosby would recall that physicians told his parents the young boy would die prematurely.

Raised under the glare of Monticello, Mosby grew up as a "Son of the South," inheritor to traditions -- some real, some invented -- at a time in history when those traditions were under attack and in decline. The two significant events in his historical life reveal some of the tendencies of Southern life, and more specifically, the State of Virginia. During his youth, the small boy frequently suffered the bullying of kids in school, but what emerged from these clashes would be a trait of Mosby's throughout his adult life, a proclivity to not back down from a physical challenge even when the odds were against him. He said later in life there never was a fight he emerged victorious from, and even in his youth, he won the begrudging respect of his peers and rivals. He later discussed one incident at school that had an effect on him, "I was seven years old when I learned to read, although I had gone a month or so to a country school in Nelson, near a post office called Murrell's Shop, where I had learned to spell. As I was so young my mother always sent a negro boy with me to the schoolhouse, and he came for me in the evening. But once I begged him to stay all day with me, and I shared my dinner with him. When playtime came, some of the larger boys put him up on a block for sale and he was knocked down to the highest bidder. I thought it was a bona fide sale and was greatly distressed at losing such a dutiful playmate. We went home together, but he never spent another day with me at the schoolhouse."

His parents, though, saw how he suffered, and more, how he needed a better education, so they moved to the larger and more populated Albemarle County, where he attended the University of Virginia. Mosby majored in Greek languages and literature, but he also earned a reputation as a supremely confident troublemaker who knew no restraints. At the University of Virginia, Mosby's friends belonged to the rowdy crew of college students who sometimes came to violent blows with each other. His crowd of friends and the parties they held earned him the notoriety of the popular students, one of whom, named George R. Turpin, attempted to bully some of them, including Mosby. Mosby's memoirs noted, "And the Colonel himself admits that he got the worst of these boyish engagements, except once, when the fight was on between him and Charles Price, of Meachem's, - and in that case they were separated before victory could perch. They also go so far as to say that he was a spirited lad, although far from 'talkative' and not far from quiet, introspective moods…His antagonist this time was George Turpin, a student of medicine in the University…Turpin had carved Frank Morrison to his taste with a pocket knife and added to his reputation by nearly killing Fred M. Wills with a rock…"

Mosby later remembered, "I did not go to Turpin's house, but he came to my boarding house, and he had sent me a message that he was coming there to 'eat me up.'" As he soon learned, Turpin picked the wrong kid to challenge in the 17 year old Mosby, who demanded to know why Turpin had said the things he had: "I hear you have been making assertions..." When the bigger kid charged him, Mosby pulled out a gun and shot Turpin in the neck. The shooting earned Mosby an expulsion from the school and a 12 month sentence that landed him in jail, but he became a cause célèbre in Virginia for protecting himself. In fact, Mosby befriended the prosecutor of the case against him, William J. Robertson, who was impressed by Mosby's interest in reading and his boast to learn the law: "That law has made a great deal out of me. I am now going to make something out of the law."[2] Mosby would go on to practice law, and he eventually had his sentence commuted to 9 months due to an outpouring of support from locals who felt his shooting in self-defense was justified, and that no Southerner had a duty to retreat in the face of an attacker who was challenging his honor. In the end, the code of honor that Mosby would profess to uphold protected him, and it supported acts of violence. Mosby would live by the codes of that tradition, both in his use of force to defend himself as a college student and during his Civil War career.

Mosby continued his individualistic ways after jail, first by marrying Mariah L. Pauline Clarke, who belonged to the Catholic Church (a minority in the Methodist and Baptist South), and by voting for the Northern Democrat Stephen A. Douglas in the 1860 presidential election. He did not hide his choices of love or politics either; when asked by someone why he went to the Catholic mass, he replied that his wife belonged to the church and his children did too. His choice for president did not deter him, nor did he back down from his proclamation of himself as a Unionist. When a secessionist confronted him, telling him that he would run Mosby through with a bayonet, Mosby responded with some Shakespeare: "Very well. We'll meet at Philippi."[3]

That said, looking back at the demographics of that election prove that Mosby was less of an anomaly than believed. In his county, the 1,178 votes for the pro-secessionist Southern Democrat John C. Breckinridge was trailed by a close 916 for candidate John Bell of the Constitutional Union party. While Bell was nowhere close to Douglas' position on the prevention of slavery's western expansion, he did represent a compromise to the South on the issue by putting the Constitution of the U.S. before all other political issues, especially slavery or abolition. In fact, the sentiments of Bell, spoken in the effort to prevent secession and national dissolution, worked to carry the states of Kentucky, Tennessee, and Virginia for him.

For his part, Mosby later explained that while he took part in militia drills, he didn't take the threat of war seriously in 1860 or even early 1861:

---

[2] Ramage, James A, *Gray Ghost: The Life of Col. John Singleton Mosby*, 24.
[3] Ramage, *Gray Ghost*, 31.

"When attending court at Abingdon in the summer of 1860 I met William
Blackford, who had been in class with me at the University and who was afterwards
a colonel of engineers on General Stuart's staff. Blackford asked me to join a
cavalry company which he was assisting to raise and in which he expected to be a
lieutenant. To oblige him I allowed my name to be put on the muster roll; but was
so indifferent about the matter that I was not present when the company organized.
William E. Jones was made captain. He was a graduate of West Point and had
resigned from the United States army a few years before. Jones was a fine soldier,
but his temper produced friction with his superiors and greatly impaired his
capacity as a commander.

There were omens of war at this time, but nobody realized the impending danger.
Our first drill was on January Court Day, 1861. I borrowed a horse and rode up to
Abingdon to take my first lesson. After the drill was over and the company had
broken ranks, I went to hear John B. Floyd make a speech on the condition of the
times. He had been Secretary of War and had lately resigned. Buchanan, in a history
of his administration, said that Floyd's resignation had nothing to do with secession,
but he requested it on account of financial irregularities he had discovered in the
War Department."

Virginians had been debating for months whether to secede or not, and everybody realized
Virginia was one of the most vital states in the Union due to its location. By being situated
between the North and South, its culture and economy were also blended between the two
sections, as reflected by the fact that neither secessionists nor those in the peace camp could
successfully establish their way on the eve of the war. A secession convention in February had
already failed, as did a Peace Convention. At the secession convention, a resolution dissolving
Virginia's ties to the Union was rejected by a vote of 88-45, and it was resolved that the
remaining slave states in the Union instead try to figure out a way to bring back the Confederate
states into the Union peacefully.

However, once the fighting at Fort Sumter made clear that military force would be used by the
North and that Lincoln would use force to quell the rebellion, Virginia decided to secede. Given
Virginia's location, it would also have been inevitable that Union soldiers would use its land to
wage war against the Deep South. As one Virginia newspaper put it on April 19, 1861, "Mr.
Lincoln may try the experiment of coercion to this extent. It will probably only drive all the
Border States to secession, and succeed in establishing the permanent division of the Union by
the slave line."

By that point, Virginians had begun to think of their state as distinctive from the North, and the
sectionalism of mid-19th century arose mostly due to a breakdown in the two party political
system. The ideologies of the Jacksonian Democrats and the neo-Federalist Whig parties had

worked for a generation and patched together the differences between the two parties. However, as the debate over slavery intensified, the North grew increasingly hostile over the dominance of the presidency by Southerners, and there was a widespread belief that the South would seek to spread slavery to the west and even possibly into the North. The slavery debate dissolved the Whigs, divided the Democrats, and created the Republicans, all of which allowed Abraham Lincoln to be elected.

Even before secession happened, the South turned to culture to explain its differences with the North, in part to justify its perceived superiority to the North and support the reasons for why the South faced such intense hostility. The antebellum South's notion of culture had its origins in the migration patterns and the origins of settlers from Europe, since it was settled by English from the southern and western counties of England. That territory was known for its manorial estates and overgrown rural plantations, which also explained why men like Mosby grew up as accomplished horsemen. The cavaliers of England ultimately settled Virginia, and their descendants modeled themselves after their cavalier ancestors. The Virginia colony that became the Old Dominion emulated much of its cultural heritage after the leadership of the English noble Thomas Berkeley, who served as governor of the royal colony and gave Virginia much of its self-styled characteristics as a hierarchical and highly stratified society, where men played hard, worked little, defended a woman's honor, ruled the family as a patriarch, and above all, conformed to an idea called *hegemonic liberty* that explained the freedom of a man as a reward for his social ascent.

Berkeley

Chapter 2: Fighting for the South

Mosby

"I rarely rested more than a day at a time." – John Mosby

Mosby belonged to the class of men and women who called themselves Unionists until the moment of Virginia's secession arrived on January 19, 1861. Called to defend their state (or their country, as Robert E. Lee famously intoned), Mosby donned a Confederate uniform and took his militia drills with the Washington Mounted Rifles seriously. When asked later why he would fight for the South despite opposing slavery, he replied, "I am not ashamed of having fought on the side of slavery—a soldier fights for his country—right or wrong—he is not responsible for the political merits of the course he fights in ... The South was my country." He would also explain this way of thinking in his memoirs by referencing Lee's decision to join the Confederacy: "When Lee resigned his commission to join the forces of his native State, he acted, as nearly every soldier acts, from personal sympathy with the combatants, and not on any legal theory of right and wrong. On the day when he resigned, he wrote his sister that he could not draw his sword against his family, his neighbors, and his friends. On the previous day, he happened to go into a store in Alexandria to pay a bill. His heart was burdened with a great sorrow, and he uttered these words, which the merchant wrote down in his journal - they still stand there to-day: 'I must say that I am one of those dull creatures that cannot see the good of secession.'"

Thus, on May 30, 1861, Mosby marched with his colleagues to the defense of Richmond, which was now the Confederate capital. Writing home to Pauline, and telling her to kiss their children for him, the frail soldier found another love: soldiering. More importantly, he found a mentor in Captain Jones, who "taught Mosby the importance of vigilance, showed him how to enforce discipline fairly, and by example demonstrated that the men appreciated efficient administration."[4] Jones also got Mosby and the men other important belongings: "At Richmond, Captain Jones, who stood high with those in authority, had procured Sharp carbines for us. We considered this a great compliment, as arms were scarce in the Confederacy. We had been furnished with sabres before we left Abingdon, but the only real use I ever heard of their being put to was to hold a piece of meat over a fire for frying. I dragged one through the first year of the war, but when I became a commander, I discarded it. The sabre and lance may have been very good weapons in the days of chivalry, and my suspicion is that the combats of the hero of Cervantes were more realistic and not such burlesques as they are supposed to be. But certainly the sabre is of no use against gunpowder."

Mosby discussed some of his early activities in his unit, and how they helped him get used to being a soldier:

"My first night in camp I was detailed as one of the camp guards. Sergeant Tom Edmonson - a gallant soldier who was killed in June, 1864 - gave me the countersign and instructed me as to the duties of a sentinel. For two hours, in a cold wind, I walked my round and was very glad when my relief came and I could go to rest on my pallet of straw. The experience of my first night in camp rather tended to chill my military ardor and was far more distasteful than picketing near the enemy's lines on the Potomac, which I afterwards did in hot and cold weather, very cheerfully; in fact I enjoyed it. The danger of being shot by a rifleman in a thicket, if not attractive, at least kept a vidette awake and watching. At this time I was the frailest and most delicate man in the company, but camp duty was always irksome to me, and I preferred being on the outposts. During the whole time that I served as a private - nearly a year - I only once missed going on picket three times a week. The single exception was when I was disabled one night by my horse falling over a cow lying in the road...We were sent, within a few days, to another camping ground, where we had plank sheds for shelter and where we drilled regularly. Several companies of infantry shared the camp with us. Once I had been detailed for camp guard and, having been relieved just as the company went out to drill, I saddled my horse and went along. I had no idea, that it was a breach of discipline to be doing double duty, until two men with muskets came up and told me that I was under arrest for it. I was too proud to say a word and, as my time had come, I went again to walking my rounds. Once after that, when we were in camp on Bull Run, I was talking at night with the Colonel in his tent and did not hear the bugle sounded for roll call. So a lieutenant, who happened to be in command, ordered me, as a

---

[4] Ramage, *Gray Ghost*, 34.

penalty, to do duty the rest of the morning as a camp guard. He knew that my absence from roll call was not wilful but a mistake. I would not make any explanation but served my tour of duty. These were the only instances in which I was punished when a private."

Mosby's introduction to J.E.B. Stuart also proved a momentous occasion because it led to the scouting activities that Mosby would have in some of the war's initial battles of importance, and that in turn allowed him to act independently later in the war. Mosby began work as a scout for Stuart at the First Battle of Bull Run and continued during McClellan's ill-fated Peninsula Campaign in 1862, including fighting at the critical Battle of the Seven Pines. He wrote home about the war's first major land battle at Bull Run:

"My dearest Pauline:

I telegraphed and wrote you from Manassas early the next morning after the battle. We made a forced march from Winchester to get to Manassas in time for the fight, - travelled two whole days and one night without stopping (in the rain) and getting only one meal. We arrived the morning before the fight. It lasted about ten hours and was terrific. When we were first brought upon the field we were posted as a reserve just in rear of our artillery and directly within range of the hottest fire of the enemy. For two hours we sat there on our horses, exposed to a perfect storm of grapeshot, balls, bombs, etc. They burst over our heads, passed under our horses, yet nobody was hurt. I rode my horse nearly to death on the battlefield, going backward and forward, watching the enemy's movements to prevent their flanking our command. When I first got on the ground my heart sickened. We met Hampton's South Carolina legion retreating. I thought the day was lost and with it the Southern cause. We begged them, for the honor of their State, to return. But just then a shout goes up along our lines. Beauregard arrives and assures us that the day will be ours. This reanimated the troops to redouble their efforts...

The fight would not have been half so long had it been an open-field one, but the Yankees were protected by a thick pine woods, so that it was almost impossible to get at them with the cavalry. They never once stood to a clash of the bayonet - always broke and ran. In the evening, when they gave way, the order was given to charge them. We were then in the distant part of the field. In a moment we were in full pursuit, and as we swept on by the lines of our infantry, at full speed, the shouts of our victorious soldiers rent the air. We pursued them for six or eight miles, until darkness covered their retreat. The whole road was blocked up with what they abandoned in their flight. All our regiment (in fact, nearly all the soldiers) now have splendid military overcoats which they took. I have provided myself very well. We took every piece of their artillery from them - 62 pieces - among them, one of the finest batteries in the world. Their total loss cannot be less than 5000. Our company is now equipped with Yankee tents, (I am writing under one). We are also eating Yankee provisions, as they left enough to feed the army a long time…"[5]

Mosby's memoirs of his participation as a scout in the First Virginia Cavalry commanded by Stuart is especially poignant in his recognition that Southern supremacy in horsemanship was partly responsible for the Confederacy's victory in the battle. The Union generals McDowell and Patterson, as Mosby points out in his memoirs, did not have cavalry, or at least not effective horse-fighters, while Stuart, who was responsible for the prevention of Union armies linking up during the fight, grasped the importance of using cavalry as attackers in their own right. Not only did the Union generals not have the benefit of cavalry acting as infantry auxiliaries, but even the most basic intelligence gathering was unavailable to their men on the field. Mosby grasped this fact and its importance.

Mosby was also impressed by the gallant appearance of Stuart, who was only about 7 years older than him. Stuart realized that he had a talented and inventive scout in Mosby, and in his first services for Stuart, Mosby could see that Stuart planned to use cavalry as more than picket-scouts that rode at the head of an army. "In his work on the outposts Stuart soon showed that he possessed the qualities of a great leader of cavalry. He never had an equal in such service. He discarded the old maxims and soon discovered that in the conditions of modern war the chief functions of cavalry are to learn the designs and to watch and report the movements of the enemy."[6]

---

[5] *The Memoirs of John S. Mosby*, http://docsouth.unc.edu/fpn/mosby/mosby.html, 51-52.
[6] *The Memoirs of John S. Mosby*, http://docsouth.unc.edu/fpn/mosby/mosby.html, 31.

Stuart

Stuart meant to use cavalry as an offensive weapon. Rather than a mere tactical jab at an enemy, the Confederate cavalry acted with its own strategic aims to cause severe disruption to an army, which meant more than raids and theft of supplies. In Stuart's hands, horse-mounted soldiers meant to cause Union armies to change direction or their entire offensive designs, and from this, Mosby evolved his own kind of fighting style on horseback. He meant to operate deep behind enemy lines, live off the land, and spread terror and deception to the foe. Between Stuart and Mosby the principle was the same: both men recognized the challenges presented by a larger, more powerful federal army, and they sought to defeat the invasion of Virginia. In both cases, the men took advantage of the Southern familiarity and skill with the horse, and it was only natural that the Confederacy would have the better cavalries. It was also followed the natural progression of warfare that the Southerners would choose to raid and attack using deception. The overmatched South, which lacked both population and war materials, had no other recourse.

Chapter 3: The Peninsula Campaign

After First Bull Run, Mosby continued to fight under Stuart, who had grown to trust his intelligence-gathering abilities at Manassas. All the while, Mosby continued to develop his ability as a raider and partisan. Of course, the North was busy planning as well, and the North's General-in-Chief, George B. McClellan, planned to capture Richmond, the Confederate capital. McClellan chose an indirect strategy to achieve this objective, hoping to limit the Confederate ability to fortify the city by the capture of the forts, towns, and waterways on the Virginia peninsula. Using his Army of the Potomac in an amphibious operation, McClellan would advance by land and sea, using the navy as his flanks while he marched up the Virginian peninsula toward Richmond. In other words, his army would not be covering Washington D.C. to the north.

McClellan

McClellan had already faced a number of issues in planning the campaign even before reaching the jump-off point. The first option for the landing spot (Urbana) had been scrapped, and there was bickering over the amount of troops left around Washington without the Army of the Potomac fighting on the Overland line. Finally, in March of 1862, after nine months in command, General McClellan began his invasion of Virginia, initiating what would become known as the "Peninsula Campaign." Showing his proclivity for turning movement and grand strategy, McClellan completely shifted the theater of operations. Rather than march directly into Richmond and use his superior numbers to assert domination, he opted to exploit the Union sea dominance and move his army via an immense naval flotilla down the Potomac into Chesapeake Bay and land at Fort Monroe in Hampton, Virginia, at the southern tip of the Peninsula. In addition to his 130,000 thousand men, he moved 15,000 thousand horses and mules by this means as well. There he planned for an additional 80,000 men to join him, at which time he would advance westward to Richmond. One of the European observers likened the launch of the campaign to the "stride of a giant."

McClellan's Peninsula Campaign has been analyzed meticulously and is considered one of the grandest failures of the Union war effort, with McClellan made the scapegoat. In actuality, there was plenty of blame to go around, including Lincoln and his Administration, which was so concerned about Stonewall Jackson's army in the Shenandoah Valley that several Union armies were left in the Valley to defend Washington D.C., and even more were held back from McClellan for fear of the capital's safety.

The Administration also micromanaged the deployment of certain divisions, and after Secretary of War Edwin Stanton's decision to shut down recruiting stations in early 1862, the Confederacy's concentration of all their troops in the area meant that the Army of the Potomac was eventually outnumbered in front of Richmond. At the beginning of the campaign, however, McClellan had vastly superior numbers at his disposal, with only about 70,000 Confederate troops on the entirety of the peninsula and fewer than 17,000 between him and the Capital. McClellan was unaware of this decisive advantage, however, because of the intelligence reports he kept receiving from Allen Pinkerton, which vastly overstated the number of available Confederate soldiers.

From the beginning, McClellan's caution and the narrow width of the Peninsula worked against his army. At Yorktown, which had been the site of a decisive siege during the Revolution, McClellan's initial hopes of surrounding and enveloping the Confederate lines through the use of the Navy was scuttled when the Navy couldn't promise that it'd be able to operate in the area. That allowed General John Magruder, whose Confederate forces were outmanned nearly 4-1, to hold Yorktown for the entire month of April. Magruder accomplished it by completely deceiving the federals, at times marching his men in circles to make McClellan think his army was many times larger. Other times, he spread his artillery batteries across the line and fired liberally and sporadically at the Union lines, just to give the impression that the

Confederates had huge numbers. The ruse worked, leaving the Union command thinking there were 100,000 Confederates.

As a result of the misimpressions, McClellan chose not to attack Yorktown in force, instead opting to lay siege to it. In part, this was due to the decisive advantage the Union had in siege equipment, including massive mortars and artillery. The siege successfully captured Yorktown in early May with only about 500 casualties, but Magruder bought enough time for General Joseph E. Johnston to march south and confront McClellan on the Peninsula. During the Civil War, one of the tales that was often told among Confederate soldiers was that Johnston was a crack shot who was a better bird hunter than just about everyone else in the South. However, as the story went, Johnston would never take the shot when asked to, complaining that something was wrong with the situation that prevented him from being able to shoot the bird when it was time. The story is almost certainly apocryphal, but it was aptly used to demonstrate the Confederates' frustration with a man who everyone regarded as a capable general. Johnston was never badly beaten in battle, but he had a habit of strategically withdrawing until he had nowhere left to retreat, ultimately cementing his reputation as being too cautious.

Johnston

At this time, Stuart's First Virginia Cavalry was under the command of General Joseph E. Johnston, and Mosby served in his familiar role as a scout, but he grew restive and asked Stuart to allow him to fight behind enemy lines. Meanwhile, Stuart had his own orders from Johnston, who matched McClellan's cautiousness and continued to withdraw his troops up the peninsula. The Army of the Potomac would swell to more than 120,000 soldiers, while the Confederates struggled to amass the rest of their forces of 59,000 strong, stationed at three different locations.

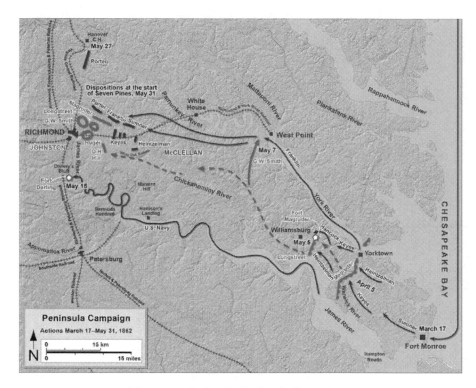

Movements during the Peninsula Campaign

Johnston continued to gradually pull his troops back to a line of defense nearer Richmond as McClellan advanced. To slow the advance, Stuart fought rearguard actions, and Mosby played a pivotal role. Usually armed with only a few men, he created feints that occupied larger numbers of Union soldiers. In a few cases, Mosby advanced with his partisans under cover of darkness and woods, fired shots at the Union positions, moved to another point and shot again, all while Mosby yelled orders in different directions, having the same few horses run back and forth. Northerners believed that Mosby commanded larger forces than he did, and the diversion caused regiments to retreat or call for reinforcements. In either case, the Union army slowed down all along the line.

Nevertheless, as McClellan advanced, the navy began moving its operations further up the James River, until it could get within 7 miles of the Confederate capital before being opposed by a Southern fort. McClellan continued to attempt to turn Johnston's flank, until the two armies were facing each other along the Chickahominy River. McClellan's Army of the Potomac got close enough to Richmond that they could see the city's church steeples.

By the end of May 1862, Stonewall Jackson had startlingly defeated three separate Northern armies in the Valley, inducing Lincoln to hold back the I Corps from McClellan. When McClellan was forced to extend his line north to link up with troops that he expected to be sent overland to him, Johnston learned that McClellan was moving along the Chickahominy River. It was at this point that Johnston got uncharacteristically aggressive. Johnston had run out of breathing space for his army, and he believed McClellan was seeking to link up with McDowell's forces. Moreover, about a third of McClellan's army was south of the river, while the other parts of the army were still north of it, offering Johnston an enticing target. Therefore he drew up a very complex plan of attack for different wings of his army, and struck at the Army of the Potomac at the Battle of Seven Pines on May 31, 1862.

Like McDowell's plan for First Bull Run, the plan proved too complicated for Johnston's army to execute, and after a day of bloody fighting little was accomplished from a technical standpoint. At one point during the Battle of Seven Pines, Confederates under General James Longstreet marched in the wrong direction down the wrong road, causing congestion and confusion among other Confederate units and ultimately weakening the effectiveness of the massive Confederate counterattack launched against McClellan. By the time the fighting was finished, nearly 40,000 had been engaged on both sides, and it was the biggest battle in the Eastern Theater to date (second only to Shiloh at the time). Although the Army of the Potomac didn't lose the battle, McClellan was rattled by the attack, and Johnston was seriously wounded during the fighting, resulting in military advisor Robert E. Lee being sent to assume command of the Army of Northern Virginia. McClellan confided to his wife, "I am tired of the sickening sight of the battlefield, with its mangled corpses & poor suffering wounded! Victory has no charms for me when purchased at such cost." Around the same time, Mosby discussed the battle with his own wife, "I went down over the battlefield yesterday. Our men were all among the enemy's tents, which were still standing, their camp kettles on the fire, etc. We whipped them in their fortifications. . . . General Lee is now in command, General Johnston being wounded. . . . There is so much confusion in Richmond that I do not know whether I can get your memorandum filled to-day. There is nothing like a panic, everybody being engaged in preparing to take care of the wounded."

From his first day in command, Lee faced a daunting challenge. McClellan had maneuvered nearly 100,000 troops to within seven miles of Richmond, three Union units were still trying to close in on General Jackson's Confederates in Virginia's Shenandoah Valley, and a fourth Union army was camped on the Rappahannock River ostensibly ready to come to McClellan's aid. On June 12, as McClellan sat on Richmond's eastern outskirts waiting for reinforcements, Lee began to ring the city with troop entrenchments. Realizing that McClellan's flank appeared to be exposed, Lee tasked Stuart with assessing whether the Union army had any real protection north and west of the exposed flank. Stuart suggested that his men circumnavigate McClellan's army, to which Lee responded with deference that would become his trademark and a symbol of his trust in his subordinates. Lee gave Stuart vague orders: "You will return as soon as the object of your expedition is accomplished, and you must bear constantly in mind, while endeavoring to execute the general purpose of your mission, not to hazard unnecessarily your command or to attempt what your judgment may not approve; but be content to accomplish all the good you can without feeling it necessary to obtain all that might be desired. I recommend that you take only such men as can stand the expedition, and that you take every means in your power to save and cherish those you take. You must leave sufficient cavalry here for the service of this army, and remember that one of the chief objects of your expedition is to gain intelligence for the guidance of future operations."

In his memoirs, Mosby took at least some of the credit for what became Stuart's most famous ride.

> "We penetrated McClellan's lines and discovered that for several miles his right flank had only cavalry pickets to guard his line of communication with his depot at the White House on the Pamunkey. Here, it seemed to me, was an opportunity to strike a blow. McClellan had not anticipated any such move and had made no provision against it.

> On discovering the conditions, I hastened back to Stuart and found him sitting in the front yard. It was a hot day - I was tired and lay down on the grass to tell him what I had learned. A martinet would have ordered me to stand in his presence. He listened to my story and, when I had finished, told me to go to the adjutant's office and write it down. At the same time he ordered a courier to get ready to go with him to General Lee's headquarters. I did as he requested and brought him a sheet of paper with what I had written. After reading it, Stuart called my attention to its not being signed. I signed it, although I had thought he only wanted a memorandum of what I had said - General Lee had never heard of me. Stuart took the paper and went off with a courier at a gallop. As soon as he returned, orders were issued to the cavalry to be ready."

With that, Stuart embarked with 1200 troopers on a spectacular three-day, 150 mile ride in the rear of and around the entire Army of the Potomac, a mission that would require him to keep just ahead of pursuing horsemen led by Union Brig. General Philip St. George Cooke, Stuart's father-in-law. Though daunting and dangerous, Stuart and his men successfully completed the historic ride, with Stuart returning to Richmond to report to Lee on June 14 and most of his cavalry returning the following day. Stuart was able not only to report that McClellan's flank was indeed completely unguarded, he delivered 165 captured Union soldiers, 260 horses and mules, and a collection of quartermaster and ordinance supplies as well. The "ride around McClellan" proved to be a public relations sensation for Stuart, resulting in dramatic newspaper accounts, hordes of women cheering and strewing flower petals in his path when he rode through the streets of Richmond, and his face appearing on the front pages of most newspapers in both the North and South. The flamboyant officer relished every second of his ride, later writing, "There was something of the sublime in the implicit confidence and unquestioning trust of the rank and file in a leader guiding them straight, apparently, into the very jaws of the enemy, every step appearing to them to diminish the faintest hope of extrication."

Stuart also knew how to cultivate his newfound glory. When Stuart reported to General Lee, he also gave a verbal report to Virginia's governor, who rewarded him with a sword. During one visit to the governor, Stuart gave an impromptu address on the steps of the executive mansion to an assembling crowd, playfully telling them he "had been to the Chickahominy to visit some of his old friends of the United States Army, but they, very uncivilly, turned their backs upon him." The man who wrote the account of that speech also noted Stuart very conspicuously galloped off as the crowd cheered. This didn't seem to bother anyone associated with him though, as Mosby later wrote, "In his work on the outposts Stuart soon showed that he possessed the qualities of a great leader of cavalry. He never had an equal in such service. He discarded the old maxims and soon discovered that in the conditions of modern war the chief functions of cavalry are to learn the designs and to watch and report the movements of the enemy."[7]

Of course, Mosby's participation in that famous ride was also documented, including a newspaper article that asserted:

> "Appreciating the public interest in the recital of everything connected with the recent exploit of General Stuart's cavalry in his reconnaissance through the enemy's lines, we have gathered, from reliable participants in the affair, these additional particulars. After destroying the enemy's camp near the old church, Lieutenant John S. Mosby, aid to General Stuart and who had been most daring and successful as a scout was sent on in advance, with a single [sic] guide, towards Tunstall Station, to reconnoitre and ascertain the position and force of the enemy. On his way he met two Yankees whom he took prisoners and sent to the rear in charge of his guide. Alone he pushed on and overtook a cavalryman and an artilleryman of the enemy's forces, having in charge a quartermaster's wagon and stores. Lieutenant Mosby dashed up and, drawing his pistols, demanded their surrender. The New Yorker surrendered at once, but the Pennsylvanian, beginning to fumble for his pistol, the lieutenant made a more emphatic demand for his surrender, and at the same moment compelled him to look quite closely into the muzzle of his pistol. All this time there was drawn up, not four hundred yards distant, a company of Yankee cavalry in line of battle. In a moment a bugle sounded as for a movement on him, when, anxious to secure his prisoners and stores, Lieutenant Mosby put spurs and

7   Mosby, John Singleton. *The Memoirs of Colonel John S. Mosby.*

galloped across the field, at the same time shouting to his imaginary men to follow him, when none of the Confederate cavalry were in sight and the swiftest more than a mile in the rear. The Yankees, hearing the word of command and apprehending the descent of an avalanche of Confederate cavalry upon them, broke line, each man galloping off to take care of himself. The wagon, prisoners, and stores were then secured and among them were found forty splendid Colt's pistols with holsters, besides boots, shoes, blankets, etc., etc."

With more Confederate troops swelling the ranks, Lee's army was McClellan's equal by late June, and on June 25, Lee commenced an all-out attempt to destroy McClellan's army in a series of fierce battles known as the Seven Days Battles. After a stalemate in the first fighting at Oak Grove, Lee's army kept pushing ahead, using Stonewall Jackson to attack McClellan's right. Although Stonewall Jackson was unusually lethargic during the week's fighting, the appearance of his "foot cavalry" spooked McClellan even more, and McClellan was now certain he was opposed by 200,000 men, more than double the actual size of Lee's army. It also made McClellan think that the Confederates were threatening his supply line, forcing him to shift his army toward the James River to draw supplies.

McClellan managed to keep his forces in tact while retreating to Harrison's Landing on the James River and establishing a new base of operation. Feeling increasingly at odds with his superiors, in a letter sent from Gaines' Mills, Virginia dated June 28, 1862, a frustrated McClellan wrote to Secretary of War Stanton, "If I save the army now, I tell you plainly that I owe no thanks to any other person in the Washington. You have done your best to sacrifice this army." McClellan's argument, however, flies in the face of common knowledge that he had become so obsessed with having sufficient supplies that he'd actually moved to Gaines' Mill to accommodate the massive amount of provisions he'd accumulated. Ultimately unable to move his cache of supplies as quickly as his men were needed, McClellan eventually ran railroad cars full of food and supplies into the Pamunkey River rather than leave them behind for the Confederates.

Despite the fact all of Lee's battle plans had been poorly executed by his generals, particularly Stonewall Jackson, he ordered one final assault against McClellan's army at Malvern Hill. Incredibly, McClellan was not even on the field for that battle, having left via steamboat back to Harrison's Landing. Biographer Ethan Rafuse notes McClellan's absence from the battlefield was inexcusable, literally leaving the Army of the Potomac leaderless during pitched battle, but McClellan often behaved coolly under fire, so it is likely not a question of McClellan's personal courage.

Ironically, Malvern Hill was one of the Union army's biggest successes during the Peninsula Campaign. Union artillery had silenced its Confederate counterparts, but Lee still ordered an infantry attack by D.H. Hill's division, which never got within 100 yards of the Union line. After the war, Hill famously referred to Malvern Hill, "It wasn't war. It was murder." Later that evening, as General Isaac Trimble (who is best known for leading a division during Pickett's Charge at Gettysburg) began moving his troops forward as if to attack, he was stopped by Stonewall Jackson, who asked "What are you going to do?" When Trimble replied that he was going to charge, Jackson countered, "General Hill has just tried with his entire division and been repulsed. I guess you'd better not try it."

After Malvern Hill, McClellan withdrew his army to Harrison's Landing, where it was protected by the U.S. Navy along the James River and had its flanks secured by the river itself. At this point, the bureaucratic bickering between McClellan and Washington D.C. started flaring up again, as McClellan refused to recommence an advance without reinforcements. After weeks of indecision, the Army of the Potomac was finally ordered to evacuate the Peninsula and link up with John Pope's army in northern Virginia, as the Administration was more comfortable having their forces fighting on one line instead of exterior lines. Upon his arrival in Washington, McClellan told reporters that his failure to defeat Lee in Virginia was due to Lincoln not sending sufficient reinforcements.

Chapter 4: The Gray Ghost

Mosby's daring grew during the summer of 1862, and his choice of audacious attacks on numerically superior Northern forces was in line with Southern efforts across the country. Mosby's next quests for adventure involved harassing Union general John Pope's Army of Virginia, and he was prepared to live off the land and hide among the people of the country. When the moment was fortuitous, he would ambush Pope. He recalled this moment in his memoirs: "I really thought that there was a chance to render effective service. I had served the first year of the war in a regiment of cavalry in the region which was now in Pope's department and had a general knowledge of the country. I was sure then - I am surer now - that I could make Pope pay as much attention to his rear as his front, and that I could compel him to detail most of his cavalry to guard his long line of communications, or turn his commissary department and rear over to me - which would have been perfectly satisfactory to me. There never was afterwards such a field for partisan war in Virginia. Breaking communications is the chief work for a partisan - it defeats plans and starts confusion by destroying supplies, thus diminishing the offensive strength of an army."[8]

Mosby also joked that if Pope did not mind his rear, then Mosby would, but instead, while staying at a farm on July 19, Mosby was captured by Union soldiers. At this juncture in Mosby's career, the Union knew little about him, and little time had been spent to allow Mosby to truly express his growing art of partisanship. Instead, he was sent north up the James River along with other prisoners. Immediately, Mosby the scout sprung back to life and sensed an opportunity to strike a blow against the North. After he saw loaded troop transports in the James River, he knew

---

[8] *Memoirs of John S. Mosby*, http://docsouth.unc.edu/fpn/mosby/mosby.html, 125-126.

they were heading either to McClellan's aid or Pope's. Mosby wrote in his memoirs, "I had been a prisoner about ten days when I was taken, with a good many prisoners, down the Potomac to Fortress Monroe. Here we waited four days for others to arrive, that we might go up the James River to the place of exchange. When we arrived at Hampton Roads, I saw a large number of transports with troops lying near. As a prisoner I kept up my habits as a scout and soon learned that they were Burnside's troops who had just come from North Carolina. If they were reinforcements for McClellan, it would indicate that he would advance again on Richmond from his new base on the James. On the other hand, if they sailed up the Chesapeake, it would show that they were going to join Pope, and that McClellan would be withdrawn from the peninsula."

Mosby set to work finding out where those ships meant to go, and he soon learned from a southern Marylander that the troops were under the command of General Ambrose Burnside; and very soon, they would go to Pope's position nearby the Potomac River. In those days of war, prisoners from both sides were regularly paroled and exchanged instead of confined, meaning paroled prisoners were simply trusted not to rejoin the fight until after they were formally exchanged. As luck and circumstance would have it, Mosby's exchange as a prisoner allowed him to continue to gather intelligence. Once released, he found a way to enter the presence of Robert E. Lee, telling him that Burnside would reinforce Pope for an attack in northern Virginia. When he met Lee, Mosby said it was like he was in the presence of a hero from Homer's *Iliad or Odyssey*, and "I felt like a man looking at a fixed star through a telescope."[9] He described the encounter in his memoirs, "We had never met before, but I was soon relieved of embarrassment; General Lee's kind, benevolent manner put me at ease. I found him looking over a map on the table. As quickly as I could, I told him that Burnside's troops had been sent to Pope. I then said that he did not know what confidence he could put in my report and told him my name and that I was on Stuart's ride around McClellan. 'Oh,' he said, 'I remember.'"

---

[9] Ramage, *Gray Ghost*, 53.

Lee

In the next few days, Mosby's scout work proved true and Lee's trust was won, as McClellan halted his advance, unbeknownst to Lee, on Lincoln's orders. Lee and his army had pushed McClellan's Army of the Potomac away from Richmond, but there was little time for celebration in July 1862. While McClellan was trying to extricate his army from a tricky spot on the Virginian Peninsula, about 50,000 Union soldiers were menacing the Confederates in Northern Virginia, outnumbering Lee's army. If McClellan's Army of the Potomac linked up with the army now being gathered in Northern Virginia, they would vastly outnumber Lee and begin yet another drive toward Richmond. For Lee, the best option (and it was hardly a good one) was to try to prevent the two Union armies from linking up, and the only way to do that would be to inflict a decisive defeat upon the army in Northern Virginia before it was joined by McClellan's men. Thus, even before McClellan had completely withdrawn his troops, Lee sent Jackson northward to intercept the new army President Abraham Lincoln had placed under Maj. General John Pope, which was formed out of the scattered troops in the Virginia area, including those who Stonewall Jackson had bedeviled during the Valley Campaign. Pope had successfully commanded Union soldiers in victories at Island No. 10 and during the Siege of Corinth, earning himself a promotion to Major General in March 1862.

Pope

When Pope's army fell back to Manassas to confront Jackson, his wing of Lee's army dug in along a railroad trench and took a defensive stance. The Second Battle of Manassas or Bull Run was fought August 28-30, beginning with the Union army throwing itself at Jackson the first two days. While Jackson's men defended themselves the first two days, Lee used Longstreet's wing on August 30 to deliver a devastating flank attack before reinforcements from the retreating Army of the Potomac could reach the field. Longstreet's attack swept Pope's army off the field. Fought on the same ground as the First Battle of Manassas nearly a year earlier, the result was the same: a decisive Confederate victory that sent Union soldiers scrambling back to the safety of Washington.

For Mosby, Second Manassas was the beginning of Lee trusting him as a source of intelligence, and Lee would say later that he wished he had "a hundred more men like Mosby." Stuart, who had struggled to placate Mosby's ambitions, now relented and allowed him to begin operations behind enemy lines. Mosby wrote home to Pauline about the Confederacy's good fortunes at the end of 1862 and also described the genesis of exploits that would earn him the name "Gray Ghost."

"My dearest Pauline:

Enclosed I send a copy of my report to General Stuart of my scout down to Manassas when with nine men I stampeded two or three thousand Yankees...General Lee sent me a message expressing his gratification at my success. I believe I have already written of my trip around McClellan at Catlett's Station, when I saw him leave his army at the time he was superseded by Burnside...

The situation is now changed. McClellan and Pope have been driven from Virginia, and Burnside has met a bloody repulse at Fredericksburg. The two hostile armies are in winter quarters on the Rappahannock, and the pickets on opposite banks have declared a truce and are swapping coffee and tobacco. Occasionally a band on the Northern bank plays a favorite Southern air and soon, in response, the strain of the Star Spangled Banner comes from our side. The cavalry is not used for picketing and has been sent to the rear to be more convenient to forage.

When he returned, Stuart let me stay behind a few days with six men to operate on the enemy's outposts. He was so satisfied with our success that he let me have fifteen men to return and begin my partisan life in northern Virginia - which closed with the war. That was the origin of my battalion. On January 24, 1863, we crossed the Rappahannock and immediately began operations in a country which Joe Johnston had abandoned a year before. It looked as though I was leading a forlorn hope, but I was never discouraged. In general my purpose was to threaten and harass the enemy on the border and in this way compel him to withdraw troops from his front to guard the line of the Potomac and Washington. This would greatly diminish his offensive power. General "Joe" Hooker said before a committee of Congress that we created so much anxiety that the planks on the bridge across the Potomac were taken up every night to prevent us from carrying off the Government."[10]

---

[10] *Memoirs of John S. Mosby*, http://docsouth.unc.edu/fpn/mosby/mosby.html, 147-150.

A picture of Mosby's Rangers.

Mosby clamored for his own command from Stuart and Lee, but his ally would be the new secretary of war of the Confederacy, who shared his belief in the potential of guerrilla operations, or as Stuart called it, *petite guerre* ("people's war.") With that, Mosby was granted the 43rd Battalion Virginia Cavalry in June of 1863. Ironically, Lee's insistence that Mosby leave the sway of irregular combat and join the ranks of the army for the purposes of a more centralized command over guerillas accounts for a great deal of reason for the creation of the 43rd. From Mosby's first days of participation in war, he had chafed against the orders of men he considered inept and actually left his unit after First Manassas for the reason of not earning a promotion. But now, Lee and Stuart both recognized his professional ambition, suggesting that if he commanded a professional military unit that was organized, led, and accountable to and by the Confederate army, he could escape the doldrums of a rank (captain) that consigned him to take orders from higher ranks.

Of course, what they really appreciated was Mosby's effectiveness. In his operations behind enemy lines, such as a fight at Miskel's Farm in early 1863, Mosby effectively utilized the revolver against cavalry six times the size of his forces. While Union cavalry fought the traditional way, getting close to swing their saber at the enemy, Mosby saw that riders with two Colt .45 revolvers could defeat and rout a larger force. Amazingly, the Union cavalry never adapted to his tactics, which emboldened Mosby to take more chances behind enemy lines.

Realizing that he could sneak into areas controlled by larger forces through this careful entry by way of stealth and surprise, Mosby began attempting to attack Union positions that fell into a condition some called "headquarterism," where commanders would shack up in a building under the assumption that their superior numbers could prevent a covert operation from reaching their position. This would also be the source of Mosby's most famous operation during the war.

Believing he could fight his way out of any predicament, Mosby undertook a mission that would serve as his greatest success, add to his infamy in the North and create more of the legend that endures today. In March 1863, Mosby saw a chance to raid Fairfax County courthouse in Virginia, used as the headquarters of the Union army of that district. Not only did Mosby know that three Union army officers slept in the courthouse, he also knew of a gap in the pickets that guarded the position, which would allow him to sneak in undetected. Through deceit and stealth, Mosby entered the courthouse and entered the room of the people sleeping there, one of whom was Brig. General Edwin Stoughton. Mosby recalled the episode in his memoirs:

> "When the squads were starting around to gather prisoners and horses, Joe Nelson brought me a soldier who said he was a guard at General Stoughton's headquarters. Joe had also pulled the telegraph operator out of his tent; the wires had been cut. With five or six men I rode to the house, now the Episcopal rectory, where the commanding general was. We dismounted and knocked loudly at the door. Soon a window above was opened, and some one asked who was there. I answered, "Fifth New York Cavalry with a dispatch for General Stoughton." The door was opened and a staff officer, Lieutenant Prentiss, was before me. I took hold of his nightshirt, whispered my name in his ear, and told him to take me to General Stoughton's room. Resistance was useless, and he obeyed. A light was quickly struck, and on the bed we saw the general sleeping as soundly as the Turk when Marco Bozzaris waked him up. There was no time for ceremony, so I drew up the bedclothes, pulled up the general's shirt, and gave him a spank on his bare back, and told him to get up. As his staff officer was standing by me, Stoughton did not realize the situation and thought that somebody was taking a rude familiarity with him. He asked in an indignant tone what all this meant. I told him that he was a prisoner, and that he must get up quickly and dress.
>
> I then asked him if he had ever heard of 'Mosby', and he said he had. 'I am Mosby,' I said. 'Stuart's cavalry has possession of the Court House; be quick and dress.'
>
> He then asked whether Fitz Lee was there. I said he was, and he asked me to take him to Fitz Lee - they had been together at West Point. Two days afterwards I did deliver him to Fitz Lee at Culpeper Court House. My motive in trying to deceive Stoughton was to deprive him of all hope of escape and to induce him to

dress quickly. We were in a critical situation, surrounded by the camps of several thousand troops with several hundred in the town. If there had been any concert between them, they could easily have driven us out; but not a shot was fired although we stayed there over an hour."[11]

Stoughton

Mosby and his men escaped with their prisoners, whom they released later in exchange for Confederates of their own. Union newspapers were aghast at Mosby's success, while the Confederate press celebrated the man they, and their Yankee opponents, had begun to call the "Gray Ghost."

Despite these kinds of successes, Lee and Stuart urged Mosby to embrace more traditional war and acquire formal army promotions, mostly in order to curb the larger problem of partisan lawlessness that had broken out since the Confederacy's passage of the Partisan Act (which permitted irregular guerrillas to keep stolen Union property). That act generated its own legitimacy to Mosby, for his command of the 43rd and rise in rank was essentially reliant upon the Southern government's recognition and support of organizing and paying guerrilla units. These units were then on their own to fight and secure their own payment in the form of stolen Northern goods.

The dilemma Mosby faced by remaining a partisan explained why he supported the Partisan

---

[11] *Memoirs of John S. Mosby*, http://docsouth.unc.edu/fpn/mosby/mosby.html, 174-176.

Act, specifically his embrace of the tactics of partisanship. For one, as he told Lee (and the general finally acquiesced), Mosby counted on plunder to pay his rangers. Losing that ability would compromise his command and ruin his ability to motivate his men. The second reason for his endorsement of partisanship was largely personal and bordered on his idea of professionalism, though what exactly he defined as professional looked strange to most military people. Yet while his approach to leading his men was largely unorthodox - he rarely drilled them, made them practice shooting, and held elections of officers - this style spoke to his own individualism. Marching and following orders for the sake of tradition and hierarchy did not sit well with his men, nor him.

For a society that was as stratified as Virginia's was, bound by traditions and deference to authority, the existence of Mosby and his men may seem like a paradox, but Southern partisans across the country thrived during the Civil War, notably William Quantrill's Raiders in Missouri and Kentucky. Given the strength of the Union army and the widespread power of the North, irregular warfare appealed to a lot of young men whose partisanship produced a type of war that was personal, retaliatory, and violent.

This type of warfare lacked the idea of decorum that most armies of the time followed, but at the same time, the North's advantages made partisans like Mosby valuable to the South because their style of combat could subsist off the enemy's supplies. Mosby would become one of the first partisans in the war to attack a train, and his successes fueled the belief (often mistakenly) that acts of courage could negate any of the advantages of foes. His dispatch to Stuart revealed his thoughts and intentions, along with the nature of battle:

> "[Dated June 6, 1863] Last Saturday morning I captured a train of twelve cars on the Virginia and Alexandria Railroad loaded with supplies for the troops above. The cars were fired and entirely consumed. . . . Having destroyed the train, I proceeded some distance back, when I recognized the enemy in a strong force immediately in my front. One shell which exploded in their ranks sufficed to put them to flight. After going about a mile further, the enemy were reported pursuing. Their advance was again checked by a shot from the howitzer. In this way we skirmished for several miles, until seeing the approach of their overwhelming numbers and the impossibility of getting off the gun, I resolved to make them pay for it as dearly as possible. Taking a good position on a hill commanding the road we awaited their onset. They came up quite gallantly, not in dispersed order, but in columns of fours, crowded in a narrow lane. At eighty yards we opened on them with grape and following this up with a charge of cavalry, we drove them half a mile back in confusion. Twice again did they rally and as often were sent reeling back. At last our ammunition became exhausted, and we were forced to abandon the gun. We did not then abandon it without a struggle, and a fierce hand to hand combat ensued in which, though overpowered

by numbers, many of the enemy were made to bite the dust. In this affair I had only 48 men - the forces of the enemy were five regiments of cavalry. My loss, one killed - Captain Hoskins, a British officer who fell when gallantly fighting, - four wounded. It is with pleasure I recommend to your attention the heroic conduct of Lieutenant Chapman and Privates Mountjoy and Beattie, who stood by their gun until surrounded by the enemy."[12]

---

[12] *Memoirs of John S. Mosby*, http://docsouth.unc.edu/fpn/mosby/mosby.html, 197-198.

A picture of Mosby taken during the war.

Chapter 5: Mosby's Confederacy

During the first weeks of summer of 1863, as Stuart screened the army and completed several well-executed offenses against Union cavalry, many historians think it likely that he had already planned to remove the negative effect of Brandy Station by duplicating one of his now famous circumnavigating rides around the enemy army. But as Lee began his march north through the Shenandoah Valley in western Virginia, it is highly unlikely that is what he wanted or expected.

Before setting out on June 22, the methodical Lee gave Stuart specific instructions as to the role he was to play in the Pennsylvania offensive: as the "Eyes of the Army" he was to guard the mountain passes with part of his force while the Army of Northern Virginia was still south of the Potomac River, and then cross the river with the remainder of his army and screen the right flank of Confederate general Richard Stoddert Ewell's Second Corps as it moved down the Shenandoah Valley, maintaining contact with Ewell's army as it advanced towards Harrisburg.

But instead of taking the most direct route north near the Blue Ridge Mountains, Stuart chose a much more ambitious course of action.

Stuart decided to march his three best brigades (under Generals Hampton and Fitzhugh Lee, and Col. John R. Chambliss) between the Union army and Washington, north through Rockville to Westminster, and then into Pennsylvania--a route that would allow them to capture supplies along the way and wreak havoc as they skirted Washington. In the aftermath, the *Washington Star* would write: "The cavalry chief [Stuart] interpreted his marching orders in a way that best suited his nature, and detached his 9000 troopers from their task of screening the main army and keeping tabs on the Federals. When Lee was in Pennsylvania anxiously looking for him, Stuart crossed the Potomac above Washington and captured a fine prize of Federal supply wagons . . . ."[13]

But to complicate matters even more, as Stuart set out on June 25 on what was probably a glory-seeking mission, he was unaware that his intended path was blocked by columns of Union infantry that would invariably force him to veer farther east than he or Lee had anticipated. Ultimately, his decision would prevent him from linking up with Ewell as ordered and deprive Lee of his primary cavalry force as he advanced deeper and deeper into unfamiliar enemy territory. According to Halsey Wigfall (son of Confederate States Senator Louis Wigfall) who was in Stuart's infantry, "Stuart and his cavalry left [Lee's] army on June 24 and did not contact [his] army again until the afternoon of July 2, the second day of the [Gettysburg] battle."[14]

---

[13]   Stepp, John W. & Hill, William I. (editors), *Mirror of War, the Washington Star reports the Civil War*. Page 199.
[14]   Eaton, Clement. *Jefferson Davis*. Page 178.

However, Stuart was defended by Mosby in his memoirs:

> "Lee's report on the Gettysburg campaign was published immediately and made a deep and almost indelible impression. It is really a lawyer's brief and shows the skill of the advocate in the art of suppression and suggestion. Stuart's report, dated August 20, 1863, is a respectful answer, but it was buried in the confederate archives. General Lee made a more elaborate report, in January, 1864, which repeated the implications of the first in regard to the cavalry, but contradicted what it said about his orders for the concentration at Gettysburg. Of course, he knew his own orders as well in July as in January.

> Now the essence of the complaint against Stuart is that the cavalry - the eyes of an army - were improperly absent; that the Confederate army was ordered by Lee to Gettysburg, and, Colonel Marshall and Lee's Assistant Adjutant General, Colonel Walter Taylor, said, and the report implies, ran unexpectedly against the enemy. But the charge falls to the ground when Lee's second report admits that the army was not ordered to Gettysburg, and that the force that went there was only making a reconnaissance. However, the report does not say that there was any order for a reconnaissance, or any necessity for making one. Neither does it explain why Hill did not come back to Cashtown, nor why Lee followed him to Gettysburg. Hill's report says that on the thirtieth he sent a dispatch to General Lee, telling him that the enemy held Gettysburg. A collision, then, could not be unexpected - if he went there. If, as Lee's report says, the spy brought news on the twenty-eighth that the Union army was at Frederick, it could not have been expected to stand still; nor a surprise to learn that it was moving north.

> But there is even less color to the truth or justice in the complaint, when it is known that the story that a spy diverted the army from Harrisburg is a fable, and that Hill and Heth went off without orders and without Lee's knowledge on a raid and precipitated a battle. There is a satisfactory explanation for Stuart's absence that day, but a man who has to make an explanation is always at a disadvantage."

While Stuart's role in the battle has been constantly analyzed, Mosby's role in the campaign may have helped Lee feel justified with bold and aggressive moves. Stuart's report of the Gettysburg Campaign showed how well the use of partisans and the cavalry worked for the Confederacy in the middle of 1863.

> "Maj. Mosby, with his usual daring, penetrated the enemy's lines and caught a staff-officer of Gen. Hooker - bearer of despatches to Gen. Pleasanton, commanding United States cavalry near Aldie. These despatches disclosed the fact that Hooker was looking to Aldie with solicitude, and that Pleasanton, with infantry and cavalry, occupied the place; and that a reconnaissance in force of

cavalry was meditated toward Warrenton and Culpeper. I immediately despatched to Gen. Hampton, who was coming by way of Warrenton from the direction of Beverly Ford, this intelligence, and directed him to meet this advance at Warrenton. The captured despatches also gave the entire number of divisions, from which we could estimate the approximate strength of the enemy's army. I therefore concluded in no event to attack with cavalry alone the enemy at Aldie. . . . Hampton met the enemy's advance toward Culpeper and Warrenton, and drove him back without difficulty - a heavy storm and night intervening to aid the enemy's retreat. I resumed my own position now, at Rector's crossroads, and being in constant communication with the commanding general, had scouts busily employed watching and reporting the enemy's movements, and reporting the same to the commanding general. In this difficult search the fearless and indefatigable Maj. Mosby was particularly efficient. His information was always accurate and reliable."[15]

Mosby's ability to fight this way stemmed largely from the support offered by locals, and this was the reason a region in northern Virginia was called "Mosby's Confederacy":

"Fauquier County had only a few Unionists, and in 1860 African Americans made up 51 percent of the population, 48 percent being slaves and about 3 percent free blacks. This percentage of blacks was higher than Virginia's 35 percent and greater than the Deep South states of Louisiana, Alabama, Florida, and Georgia, More than 40 percent of the white families in Fauquier owned slaves, which was considerably higher than the 25 percent in Virginia and the entire South. More than 13 percent, 128 families, owned twenty of more slaves, a greater proportion than 11 percent for Virginia and 12 percent for the South. Together, Loudoun and Fauquier had 161 gentry with 20 or more slaves, Loudoun with 165 and Fauquier with 284. Thus, both counties had 610 slave-owning families with 8 or more slaves. Not all of these families were located within Mosby's Confederacy, but they could provide assistance when he came scouting or marching through. Mosby had selected this base of operations for his people's war very effectively; he depended on a concentration of slave owners true to the Southern cause."[16]

1864 brought the brutal Overland Campaign to Virginia, as Grant and Lee's armies fought bloody stalemates that nonetheless saw the Union Army of the Potomac push south until it was laying siege to Petersburg. With little ability to win decisively on the battlefield, the South could only hope to achieve a political victory, as 1864 was a presidential election year in the Union. Lee agreed with Mosby's idea that partisans should attack simultaneously in multiple locations in northern Virginia, for the purposes preventing the Army of the Potomac from achieving a

[15] *Memoirs of John S. Mosby*, http://docsouth.unc.edu/fpn/mosby/mosby.html, 200.
[16] Ramage, *The Gray Ghost*, 101.

coordination of all its forces for an attack and capture of Richmond. The plan worked with partial success, but none so cleverly designed, and almost close to the achievement of success as the attack on Washington D.C.

Events started with a fresh round of partisan attacks on Union forces in Virginia during the late spring of 1864, and the simultaneous attack were especially disruptive, leading to accounts in the Northern press that the partisans were numerous and everywhere. Grant wanted to secure the Shenandoah Valley before attacking Richmond, but the XI Corps of the Army of the Potomac, commanded by Major General Franz Sigel, proved ineffective at this task. Following his defeat at the hands of General Breckinridge at the Battle of New Market, Sigel was replaced by Major General David Hunter. However, the real reason for Sigel's demotion can be explained by his ineffectiveness of dealing with the partisan threat under Mosby's command. Hunter was called "Black Smoke" because that was how he dealt with partisans -- he went to the source of their power, the civilian homes in Mosby's Confederacy, and burned down the properties.

Hunter

At the battle of Yellow Tavern on May 11, 1864, Jeb Stuart was mortally wounded, depriving Lee's army of its most famous cavalier. Mosby now was forced to adjust to Stuart's replacements, and as the siege of Petersburg started, Lee tasked Jubal Early with leading men towards Washington D.C. in an effort to force Grant to peel away some of his besieging forces. At the same time, however, the city was an intimidating objective:

> "By the close of the Civil War, Washington, D.C. was the most heavily fortified city in North America, perhaps even in the world. According to the report of the army's official engineer, her defenses boasted 68 enclosed forts with 807 mounted cannon and 93 mortars, 93 unarmed batteries with 401 emplacements for field guns and 20 miles of rifle

trenches plus three blockhouses. Moreover miles of military roads, a telegraphic communication system and supporting infrastructure — including headquarters buildings, storehouses and construction camps — ringed the city."[17]

The South did not have the resources, nor the ability to break through or besiege the Union capital, but Grant begrudgingly sent two corps back to the Washington. Mosby played a significant in this, using his 43rd to support Early's advance: "With 250 men, Mosby had diverted 2,800 from Washington, and that was more than eleven times his own number. With timing and an audacious midday attack [on Harper's Ferry], punctuated with the booming of the cannon and the charge of dismounted men, Mosby's 250 created the impression of 20,000 and in the enemy minds extend the invasion from to fifty miles."

Early

Mosby was used to Stuart's movements, and the two could work in tandem without communications at times, but Early did not communicate with Mosby upon his advance, which slighted Mosby; and Early's correspondence with Mosby went unread because Mosby preferred to anticipate Early's battlefield movements. Early tended to give oral directions, while Mosby expected written instructions, like Lee and Stuart had been known to do.

Mosby did cross the Potomac within sight of the Union capital, but Early was repulsed at the

[17] Cooling, B.F. and Wally Owen, "Washington's Civil War Defenses and the Battle of Fort Stevens,": http://www.civilwar.org/battlefields/fortstevens/fort-stevens-history-articles/washingtons-civil-war.html

Battle of Fort Stevens on July 11-12, 1864. Early, after the war, said in his memoirs that he put the reason for not attacking Washington on Mosby's lack of intelligence gathering, which Early requested. Mosby would later respond that he had tried to meet at Maryland Heights for the purpose of working in concert, but eventually, the disagreement between the two turned into more than an argument. Mosby later called Early his "malignant enemy."[18]

"On July 4, hearing of General Early's movement down the Valley, I moved with my command east of the Blue Ridge for the purpose of cooperating with him and crossed the Potomac at Point of Rocks, driving out the garrison (250 men, strongly fortified) and securing several prisoners and horses. As I supposed it to be General Early's intention to invest Maryland Heights, I thought the best service I could render would be to sever all communication both by railroad and telegraph between that point and Washington, which I did, keeping it suspended for two days.

As this was the first occasion on which I had used artillery [sic] the magnitude of the invasion was greatly exaggerated by the fears of the enemy, and panic and alarm spread through their territory. I desire especially to bring to the notice of the commanding general the unsurpassed gallantry displayed by Captain Richards, commanding First Squadron. Our crossing was opposed by a body of infantry stationed on the Maryland shore. Dismounting a number of sharpshooters, whom I directed to wade the river above the point held by the enemy, I superintended in person the placing of my piece of artillery in position at the same time directing Captain Richards whenever the enemy had been dislodged by the sharpshooters and artillery, to charge across the river in order to effect their capture. The enemy were soon routed and Captain Richards charged over, but before he could overtake them they had retreated across the canal, pulling up the bridge in their rear. My order had not, of course, contemplated their pursuit into their fortifications, but the destruction of the bridge was no obstacle to his impetuous valor, and hastily dismounting and throwing down a few planks on the sills, he charged across, under a heavy fire from a redoubt. The enemy fled panic stricken, leaving in our possession their camp equipage, etc. . . .

On the morning of July 6, while still encamped near the Potomac, information was received that a considerable force of cavalry was at Leesburg. I immediately hastened to meet them. At Leesburg I learned that they had gone toward Aldie, and I accordingly moved on the road to Ball's Mill in order to intercept them returning to their camp in Fairfax, which I succeeded in doing, meeting them at Mount Zion Church, and completely routing them, with a loss of about 80 of their officers and men left dead and severely wounded on the field, besides 57

---

[18] Ramage, *Gray Ghost*, 162.

prisoners. Their loss includes a captain and lieutenant killed and 1 lieutenant severely wounded; the major commanding and 2 lieutenants prisoners. We also secured all their horses, arms, etc.

My loss was 1 killed and 6 wounded - none dangerously.

After this affair the enemy never ventured, in two months after, the experiment of another raid through that portion of our district.

A few days afterward I again crossed the Potomac in cooperation with General Early, and moved through Poolesville, Md., for the purpose of capturing a body of cavalry encamped near Seneca. They retreated, however, before we reached there, leaving all their camp equipage and a considerable amount of stores. We also captured 30 head of beef cattle."[19]

Chapter 6: The End of the War

"The cavalry-camp lies on the slope

Of what was late a vernal hill,

But now like a pavement bare-

An outpost in the perilous wilds

Which ever are lone and still;

But Mosby's men are there -

Of Mosby best beware.

Great trees the troopers felled, and leaned

In antlered walls about their tents;

Strict watch they kept; 'twas Hark! and Mark!

Unarmed none cared to stir abroad

For berries beyond their forest-fence:

As glides in seas the shark,

---

[19] *Memoirs of John S. Mosby*, http://docsouth.unc.edu/fpn/mosby/mosby.html, 275-277.

Rides Mosby through green dark.

All spake of him, but few had seen

Except the maimed ones or the low;

Yet rumor made him every thing-

A farmer-woodman-refugee-

The man who crossed the field but now;

A spell about his life did cling -

Who to the ground shall Mosby bring?

The morning-bugles lonely play,

Lonely the evening-bugle calls -

Unanswered voices in the wild;

The settled hush of birds in nest

Becharms, and all the wood enthralls:

Memory's self is so beguiled

That Mosby seems a satyr's child." - "The Scout Toward Aldie," by Herman Melville.[20]

Mosby merely had to read Northern newspapers to understand the impression he had on Union soldiers in northern Virginia, and Melville's references to him were a good example of the fear Union soldiers had when they were near Mosby's Confederacy. His worst effect might have been on Union General-in-Chief Henry Halleck, because at various times during the summer of 1864, Halleck repeatedly felt the need to counter Mosby's moves for the defense of Washington. Halleck believed defending the Union capital required capturing Mosby or at least wreaking such havoc on northern Virginia that Confederates couldn't live off the land there. Grant tasked Sheridan with the scorched earth task: "Grant left no doubt as to how Sheridan was to proceed. He ordered Sheridan to "Put himself south of the enemy and follow him to the death." Grant wanted Sheridan to rely on cavalry rather than infantry, telling him, 'Let your headquarters be in the saddle.' Sheridan was to 'eat out Virginia clear and clean as far as they [soldiers] go, so that crows flying over it for the balance of the season will have to carry their provender with them.'"[21]

[20] "'The Scout Toward Aldie,' by Herman Melville," http://www.civilwar.org/education/history/on-the-homefront/literature/scout.html

Sheridan

Sheridan's main objective was to literally destroy the Shenandoah Valley, but Mosby was his second priority, and Mosby made sure Sheridan paid attention to him. Sheridan's assignment required creating a supply line to Grant, which required transporting supply wagons across Mosby's Confederacy. Given Mosby's penchant for raiding supplies and his record of success, Sheridan knew that his army would eventually face the partisans.

Even before the fight began, Mosby was already in Sheridan's head. When the first wagons were preyed upon, Sheridan responded piecemeal against the attacks, but he could merely swat at them like bothersome gnats. Tired of the loss of supplies, Sheridan used Custer and his Michigan Brigade, to hunt and kill Mosby's rangers. What followed was the most brutal episode of the war in northern Virginia.

The first blood came when Custer's men captured some of Mosby's men after the Confederate partisans had captured some Northern supplies. For the loss of wagons, Grant spelled out the solution to Mosby's depredations, saying, "The families of most of Mosby's men are known, and can be collected. I think they should be taken and kept at Fort McHenry, or some secure place, as

[21] Wukovits, John F, "George Custer and John Mosby Clash in the Shenandoah Valley," http://www.civilwar.org/battlefields/thirdwinchester/third-winchester-history-articles/john-mosby-and-george-custer.html

hostages for the good conduct of Mosby and his men."[22] Sheridan expressed some of the same fiery rage, admitting in official dispatches, "Mosby has annoyed me and captured a few wagons. We hung one and host sic of his men yesterday."[23] Days later, Sheridan made more notes of his retaliations, again in the orders, "Guerillas give me great annoyance, but I am quietly disposing of number of them" and "we have disposed of quite a number of Mosby's men." Eventually, Grant and Sheridan calmed down and came up with a different solution: arresting all males under 50 and holding them as prisoners of war. Grant also ordered the destruction of food and forage in the Shenandoah Valley, and the freeing of slaves and destroying of crops and livestock in Mosby's Confederacy.

Nonetheless, the intense fights between Mosby's command and Union cavalry continued, and it would bring about hangings and other summary executions. During an August 13 raid, Mosby's men captured 700 horses and mules, 200 men, 100 wagons, and 200 cattle, and in response, Custer, whom the Virginians called "Attila the Hun," served notice that he had no intention of being lenient. Custer targeted civilians and private property, and Mosby returned each attack with a bloody vengeance: "Custer learned that a light at a local farmhouse had served as a signal for guerrillas; so Custer ordered it and all of the surrounding homes destroyed. As his men were setting fire to the elegant residences, a group of Mosby's men led by J. G. L. William Chapman charged from an overlooking ridge, splashed through the Shenandoah River, and smacked into Custer's outfit. Chapman exhorted his men to 'Wipe them from the face of the earth! No quarter! No quarter! Take no prisoners!'"[24]

---

[22] Ramage, *Gray Ghost*, 193.
[23] Ramage, *Gray Ghost*, 193.
[24] Wukovits, John F, "George Custer and John Mosby Clash in the Shenandoah Valley," http://www.civilwar.org/battlefields/thirdwinchester/third-winchester-history-articles/john-mosby-and-george-custer.html

Custer

Custer's men fled from the counterattack, and a northern woman watched as Mosby's men executed some of the men they captured. One Union cavalryman kneeled down and prayed aloud before being shot in the head, one of 25 men executed. Given the nature of the reprisals, such atrocities ensured similar ones on the other side, and all the while, the Valley suffered. Barns were torched, and crops and livestock were burned and killed.

Custer's victory over Confederates at Opequon Creek, with the capture of 700 rebels. Sheridan saw what Custer accomplished in the Valley, knowing that for every victory, Custer employed methods that made him the most hated man in Virginia. Mosby's men possessed a new vengeance, and so terrorized northern supply trains that estimates of Union needs to protect the Army of the Potomac hovered around 500 cavalry for every wagon train. Everywhere Sheridan's supplies traveled to Grant, Union forces were drawn deeper and deeper into a morass of missing soldiers who turned up in a field with their throats slashed. Naturally, both sides thought of the other as inhumane and without morals, so the more Mosby's men raided and executed Union soldiers, the more Sheridan would order the destruction of the Valley. As one historian noted, the two sides were bringing about the worst in each other: "Invariably, warfare fought in such a brutal manner will lead to horrific atrocities. That is what happened on September 22, near the town of Front Royal, midway up the Valley. A Northern ambulance train was attacked by a group of Rangers led by Captain Sam Chapman, William's brother. Chapman's force quickly realized they were outnumbered, and in an attempt to break out, rode directly at Northern troops. After the skirmish, the mangled body of Lieutenant Charles McMaster was found in the road, riddled with bullets and trampled by horses. Northern troops swore McMaster was brutally gunned down while trying to surrender. Rangers claimed he was killed in the heat of short, intense battle after his panicky horse rode into their ranks."[25]

Custer's men used the end of engagements with the rebels as periods of demonstrative executions. After they were captured, Mosby's men would end up marched through a town, shot on the spot, or taken into the woods and hung from a tree. Guns were fired point blank into people's faces, and horses dragged unconscious boys through town until a revolver ended their lives. Gangs of Union soldiers would riot against captives, with their officers offering one final chance to tell them of Mosby's location. A refusal to divulge information led to a quick execution and a sign placed over them: "Such is the Fate of All Mosby's Gang."

The killings also became more personal as Sheridan and Custer lost colleagues they considered untouchable, such as Lieutenant John Meigs, a topographical engineer that Sheridan and Custer were fond of. In response to his killing, Union soldiers destroyed every house within a 5 mile radius of Meigs' murder. During one 5 day period, Custer turned an 85 mile strip of the Valley into a conflagration of burning barns and homes.

Not surprisingly, Mosby's response was revenge:

> "Mosby told his men to sort through prisoners until they gathered 27 of Custer's men. Facing the captives, Mosby mentioned, 'There is but one man I would rather see than you and that is your commander...I can't identify the particular men that put the ropes around the necks of my Rangers, but I have a little account to settle with General Custer anyway.'...Twenty-seven pieces of paper were placed into a hat. Seven of the pieces had numbers scrawled on them, the rest were blank. Those who drew a blank would be sent to Richmond or Libby prison, while a scrap of paper bearing a number meant death. Each prisoner was forced to reach into the hat and draw out his own fate. Any man unfortunate enough to pull out a number was walked over to the side under special guard. One Ranger grotesquely greeted them by saying, 'We'll give you a chance to stretch hemp.'"[26]

---

[25] Wukovits, John F, "George Custer and John Mosby Clash in the Shenandoah Valley," http://www.civilwar.org/battlefields/thirdwinchester/third-winchester-history-articles/john-mosby-and-george-custer.html
[26] Wukovits, John F, "George Custer and John Mosby Clash in the Shenandoah Valley,"

Mosby's men left a letter on one executed soldier that read, "These men have been hung in retaliation in equal number of Col. Mosby's men hung by order of Gen. Custer, at Front Royal. Measure for Measure." But Mosby also wrote a letter to Sheridan:

> "General: Some time in the month of September, during my absence from my command, six of my men who had been captured by your forces, were hung and shot in the streets of Front Royal, by order and in the immediate presence of Brigadier-General Custer. Since then another (captured by a Colonel Powell on a plundering expedition into Rappahannock) shared a similar fate. A label affixed to the coat of one of the murdered men declared "that this would be the fate of Mosby and all his men."
>
> Since the murder of my men, not less than seven hundred prisoners, including many officers of high rank, captured from your army by this command have been forwarded to Richmond; but the execution of my purpose of retaliation was deferred, in order, as far as possible, to confine its operation to the men of Custer and Powell. Accordingly, on the 6th instant, seven of your men were, by my order, executed on the Valley Pike - your highway of travel.
>
> Hereafter, any prisoners falling into my hands will be treated with the kindness due to their condition, unless some new act of barbarity shall compel me, reluctantly, to adopt a line of policy repugnant to humanity.
>
> Very respectfully,
>
> your obedient servant, John S. Mosby, Lieut. Colonel"[27]

Sheridan's destruction of the Valley continued until Thanksgiving 1864, though he confined his men from targeting homes, just barns and other properties. Mosby claimed that his men acted with more restraint after that, and Sheridan ordered Custer to stop the hangings. Still, the Valley would not recover for years, and Virginians referred to the time of its devastation as "The Burning."

Sheridan, now forced to fight a limited war against Mosby for fear of a return of the bloody reprisals, relied on other tricks to neutralize Mosby's power in northern Virginia. The 43rd continued to interrupt the supply lines of the Army of the Potomac, even though Lee's Army of Northern Virginia was near capitulation, and Sheridan was forced to go on the defensive, something he didn't like at all. While Sheridan's methods against the guerrillas continued to rely

http://www.civilwar.org/battlefields/thirdwinchester/third-winchester-history-articles/john-mosby-and-george-custer.html
[27] "The Memoirs of Colonel John S. Mosby," http://docsouth.unc.edu/fpn/mosby/mosby.html, 302-303.

on nightly raids and midnight searches, the continuation of attacks against Mosby failed to dislodge him or his allies. The Union army ultimately used infantry picket lines to seal the lower Valley, but that couldn't continue once the North required more infantry to engage Lee.

Other commanders used tactics learned from the wars against Native Americans west of the Mississippi River. The value of ambushes by dismounted men as a method of intercepting Mosby's raiders required five man teams to attack on roads and bypaths. The work took more than the five man teams could handle, and this method eventually failed after Mosby's me destroyed each outpost one by one. Other defensive networks, including screens of stockades with their own supporting patrols on the flanks, were more successful, but the effort required to mount the operations proved that Mosby's Confederacy continued to control northern Virginia.

Union military officers finally resorted to legal arguments by arresting men they considered irregular fighters and not protected by the law. This required finding Virginians willing to testify that Mosby's Rangers could not get protection from the Partisan Act and thus should not be treated as soldiers but as outlaws and freebooters who belonged to no formal military organization. These trials had begun in earnest during the first months of 1864, and it was ascertained from the divulgement of information by Southern witnesses that Mosby gained many of his recruits through the promise of spoils and adventure, but these admissions only proved that Mosby's power and influence was increasing in the region in 1864. Throughout the year, Sheridan had fought a successful campaign against Mosby, but most of the damage done was economic. Arresting Mosby's men and refusing to exchange prisoners could deplete Mosby's command, but he could find new recruits to fight.

As a result, Mosby's Confederacy was never truly conquered by the Union, even as they were in the process of taking Richmond. On April 2, 1865, Grant finally broke Lee's lines at Petersburg, which forced the evacuation of that city and Richmond itself. While Grant's army continued to chase Lee's retreating army westward, the Confederate government sought to escape across the Deep South. On April 4, President Lincoln entered Richmond and toured the home of Confederate President Jefferson Davis.

Fittingly, the food rations Lee moved toward did not arrive as anticipated. On April 7, 1865, Grant sent Lee the first official letter demanding Lee's surrender. In it Grant wrote, "The results of the last week must convince you of the hopelessness of further resistance on the part of the Army of Northern Virginia in this struggle. I feel it is so, and regret it as my duty to shift myself from the responsibility of any further effusion of blood by asking of you the surrender of that portion of the Confederate States army known as the Army of Northern Virginia."[28] Passing the note to General Longstreet, now his only advisor, Longstreet said, "Not yet."[29] But by the

---

[28] Horn, Stanley F. (editor). *The Robert E. Lee Reader.* Page 436.
[29] Davis, Kenneth C. *The Civil War: Everything You Need to Know About America's*

following evening during what would be the final Confederate Council of War (and after one final attempt had been made to break through Union lines), Lee finally succumbed, stating regretfully, "There is nothing left me but to go and see General Grant, and I had rather die a thousand deaths."[30]

Communications continued until April 9, at which point Lee and Grant two met at Appomattox Court House. When Mosby learned of Lee's surrender to Grant there, it hit him so hard that he claimed he broke down, commenting, "I thought I had sounded the profoundest depth of human feeling, but this is the bitterest hour of my life."[31] Melodramatics aside, Mosby's end in the war resembled his choice of warfare, because he never formally surrendered; his disbandment of the 43rd took place after a heartbroken trip through Mosby's Confederacy, perhaps knowing that one life was ending and a new one was beginning. He had talked to Union officials who were anxious for him to surrender, but he wanted Grant to accept his soldiers as regulars and deserving of equal protection for all Confederate soldiers.

Gaining that amnesty for his men was one thing, but getting amnesty for himself was another. Even after General Joseph E. Johnston surrendered his men to William Tecumseh Sherman, some urged Mosby to lead them to Richmond and kidnap the Union officers in the capital. Sensing the end, Mosby told them that any future partisan acts would now certainly be considered the acts of outlaws, given that the Confederate armies had surrendered: "Too late! It would be murder and highway robbery now. We are soldiers, not highwaymen."

Instead, he chose to disband the unit, and on that day, he addressed them:

"Fauquier County, April 21, 1865.

Soldiers -

I have summoned you together for the last time. The visions we have cherished of a free and independent have vanished, and that country is now the spoil of the conqueror. I disband your organization in preference to surrendering it to our enemies. I am no longer your Commander. After an association of more than two eventful years, I part from you with a just pride in the fame of your achievements and a grateful recollection of your generous kindness to myself. And at this moment of bidding you a final adieu, accept the assurance of my unchanging confidence and regard. Farewell!

Greatest Conflict but Never Learned. Page 402.
[30]   Davis, Kenneth C. *The Civil War: Everything You Need to Know About America's Greatest Conflict but Never Learned.* Page 402.
[31] Ramage, *Gray Ghost*, 262.

Jno. S. Mosby, Colonel, Valley Farm, Aug. 27, '65."[32]

Mosby's attempt to win a pardon for his soldiers and later for himself spoke to his belief that the men who fought for Virginia deserved the reputation and treatment of gentlemen. He felt he achieved this status through Lee's admiration for him, and despite a $5,000 bounty on his head during the war, he was ultimately paroled by Grant weeks after the war ended. Ironically, Mosby would actually work for the Republican Party later in life, and he even campaigned for Grant during Grant's presidential years. He was apt to support Grant due to his belief that the former Union general would do much to reform the relationship between the North and the South, but this understandably cost him the support of some Southerners.

Shortly after the war, Mosby was interviewed by *The Philadelphia Post*, and some of his answers to the questions illuminated how he felt about the war once it was done.

"Whom do you consider the ablest General on the Federal side?"

"McClellan, by all odds. I think he is the only man on the Federal side who could have organized the army as it was. Grant had, of course, more successes in the field in the latter part of the war, but Grant only came in to reap the benefits of McClellan's previous efforts. At the same time, I do not wish to disparage General Grant, for he has many abilities, but if Grant had commanded during the first years of the war, we would have gained our independence. Grant's policy of attacking would have been a blessing to us, for we lost more by inaction than we would have lost in battle. After the first Manassas the army took a sort of 'dry rot', and we lost more men by camp diseases than we would have by fighting."

"What is your individual opinion of Jeff Davis?"

"I think history will record him as one of the greatest men of the time. Every lost cause, you know, must have a scapegoat, and Mr. Davis has been chosen as such; he must take all the blame without any of the credit. I do not know any man in the Confederate States that could have conducted the war with the same success that he did."

"Are there any bitter feelings cherished?"

"No, not now, except those engendered since the war by the manner in which we have been treated. . . . The whole administration of affairs in Virginia is in the hands of a lot of bounty jumpers and jailbirds, and their only qualification is that they can take the iron-clad oath!" "But," he added, "they generally take anything

---

[32] "The Memoirs of Col. John S. Mosby," http://docsouth.unc.edu/fpn/mosby/mosby.html, 360.

else they can lay their hands on."

Mosby practiced law until his death in 1916, spending most of his time living in Washington, the same city he had threatened to "visit" during the Civil War and see President Lincoln. On some occasions, he was actually arrested when he left Fauquier County, one of the counties of Mosby's Confederacy, but by old age his probation no longer had any power. When those who defended Lee attempted to make Stuart the scapegoat for defeat at Gettysburg, Mosby rose up to protect Stuart's memory, and eventually, Mosby's Civil War record earned him praise from American presidents. Ironically, the man who mostly eschewed traditional combat with the Army of Northern Virginia would go on to work as an ambassador in Hong Kong and a reformist federal official in the cattle lands of Nebraska.

Mosby in old age.

Cot.Jno.S.Mosby - Lieut.Jno.S.Russell

Mosby and one of his lieutenants decades after the war.

Bibliography

Alexander, John H. Mosby's Men. New York: Neale Publishing Company, 1907. OCLC 297987971.

Allardice, Bruce S. Confederate Colonels: A Biographical Register. Columbia: University of Missouri Press, 2008. ISBN 978-0-8262-1809-4.

Barefoot, Daniel W. Let Us Die Like Brave Men: Behind the Dying Words of Confederate Warriors. Winston-Salem, NC: John F. Blair Publisher, 2005. ISBN 978-0-89587-311-8.

Boyle, William E. "Under the Black Flag: Execution and Retaliation in Mosby's Confederacy",

Military Law Review 144 (Spring 1994): p. 148ff.

Crawford, J. Marshall. Mosby and His Men. New York: G. W. Carleton, 1867. OCLC 25241469.

Jones, Virgil Carrington. Ranger Mosby. Chapel Hill: University of North Carolina Press, 1944. ISBN 0-8078-0432-0.

McGiffin, Lee. Iron Scouts of the Confederacy. Arlington Heights, IL: Christian Liberty Press, 1993. ISBN 1-930092-19-9.

Mosby, John Singleton, and Charles Wells Russell. The Memoirs of Colonel John S. Mosby. New York: Little, Brown, and Company, 1917. OCLC 1750463.

Siepel, Kevin H. Rebel: The Life and Times of John Singleton Mosby, Lincoln: University of Nebraska Press, 2008. ISBN 978-0-8032-1609-9. First published 1983 by St. Martin's Press.

Smith, Eric. Mosby's Raiders, Guerrilla Warfare in the Civil War. New York: Victoria Games, Inc., 1985. ISBN 978-0-912515-22-9.

Wert, Jeffry D. Mosby's Rangers: The True Adventure of the Most Famous Command of the Civil War. New York: Simon & Schuster, 1990. ISBN 0-671-74745-2.

Made in the USA
Coppell, TX
24 May 2021